Name: _______________   Date: _______________

I can write my name

John Smith

John Smith

I can write my name

John Smith

I can write my name

John Smith

I can write my name

John Smith

I can write my name

John Smith

I can write my name

John Smith

I can write my name

John Smith

I can write my name

John Smith

I can write my name

John Smith

I can write my name

John Smith

I can write my name

John Smith

John Smith

I can write my name

John Smith

I can write my name

John Smith

I can write my name

John Smith

I can write my name

John Smith

I can write my name

John Smith

I can write my name

John Smith

I can write my name

John Smith

I can write my name

John Smith

I can write my name

John Smith

I can write my name

John Smith

I can write my name

John Smith

I can write my name

John Smith

I can write my name

John Smith

Name: _______________   Date: _______________

I can write my name

John Smith

I can write my name

John Smith

Name: _______________   Date: _______________

I can write my name

John Smith

I can write my name

John Smith

Thank you, for your purchase. It's highly, appreciated. Continue, being great and leading, your child to greatness.

Graphic credits to pixabay